I Ching Meditations: A Woman's Book of Changes
Volume One
Adele Aldridge, PhD

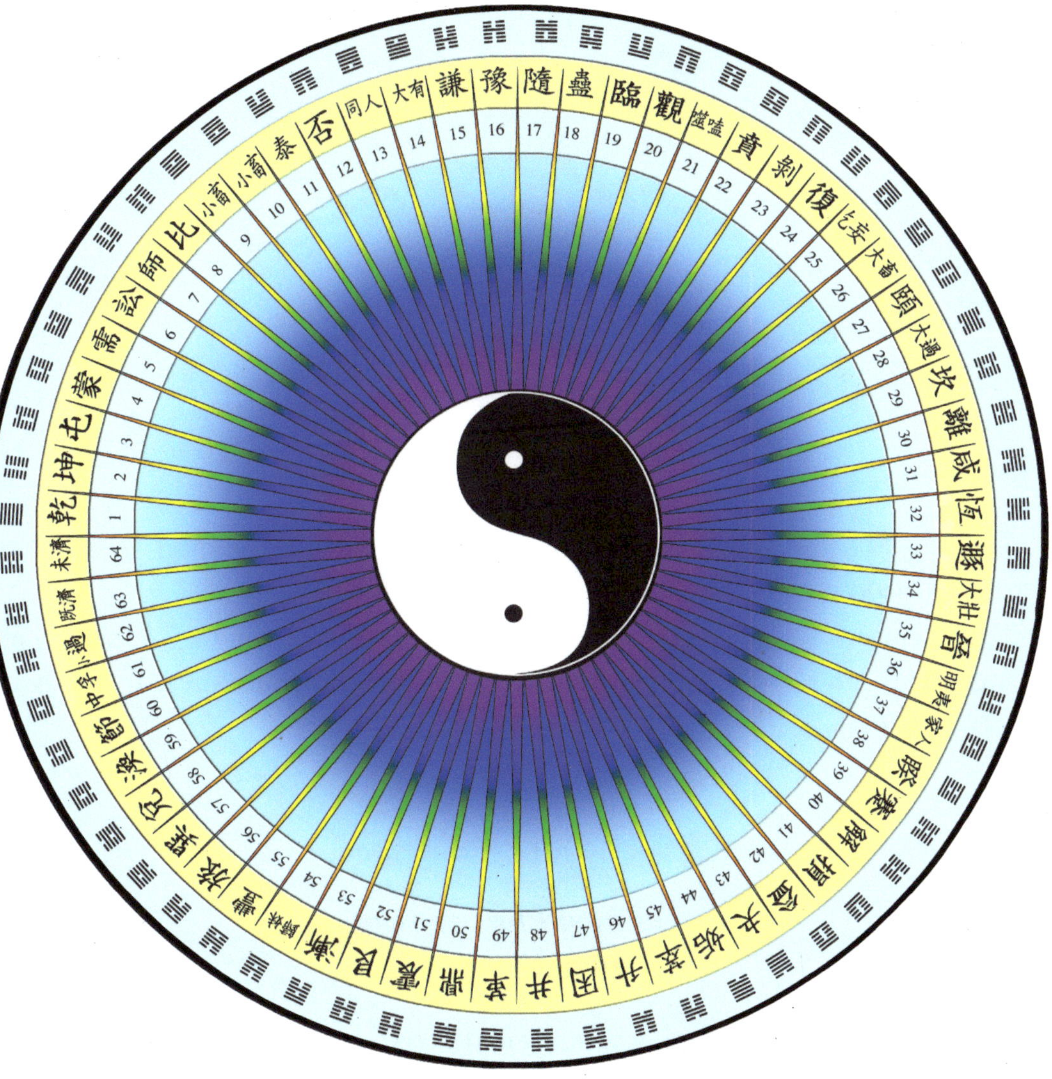

The 64 Hexagrams in Circular Arrangement

© Adele Aldridge 2012

All rights reserved

ISBN-13: 978-0615743264
ISBN-10: 0615743269

AdeleArt.com

I Ching Meditations, Volume One was originally published in 1983 in a limited edition with a Foreword by José Argüelles.

The circular image on the inside cover has been included in, Magical Mathematics by Persi Diaconsis and Ron Graham; published by Princeton University Press, 2012.

Also by Adele Aldridge:

I Ching Prescriptions
I Ching Record Book

www.adeleart.com
www.ichingmeditations.com

TABLE OF CONTENTS

Foreword by Katya Walter, PhD 4
Preface 7
Trigram • *Ch'ien* • The Creative Heaven 10
Trigram • *Chen* • The Arousing Thunder 11
Trigram • *K'an* • The Abysmal Water 12
Trigram • *Ken* • The Keeping Still Mountain 13
Trigram • *K'un* • The Receptive Earth 14
Trigram • *Sun* • The Gentle Wind & Wood 15
Trigram • *Li* • The Clinging Fire 16
Trigram • *Tui* • The Joyous Lake 17
Hexagram 1 • *Ch'ien* • The Creative 19
Hexagram 2 • *K'un* • The Receptive 27
Hexagram 3 • *Chun* • Difficulty at the Beginning 35
Hexagram 4 • *Mêng* • Youthful Folly 43
Hexagram 5 • *Hsü* • Waiting 51
Hexagram 6 • *Sung* • Conflict 59
Hexagram 7 • *Shih* • The Army 67
Hexagram 8 • *Pi* • Union 75
Hexagram 9 • *Hsiao Chu'u* • The Taming Power of the Small   83
Hexagram 10 • *Lü* • Treading 91
Hexagram 11 • *T'ai* • Peace 99
Hexagram 12 • *P'i* • Standstill 107
Hexagram 13 • *T'ung Jên* • Friendship in the Open 115
Hexagram 14 • *Ta Yu* • Possession in Great Measure 123
Hexagram 15 • *Ch'ien* • Modesty 131
Hexagram 16 • *Yü* • Enthusiasm 139
Bibliography 148
About the Author 149
About Katya Walter 149

Foreword by Katya Walter, PhD

I Ching Meditations: a Woman's Book of Changes is such a beautiful and heart-touching volume that just leafing through its pages will introduce you to it more grippingly than anything I can say about it. The wonder of it speaks for itself.

This illustrated version of the *I Ching* is Volume One of a four-part series. It is glorious in its colorful representation of the first sixteen hexagrams. The author illustrates not only each hexagram, but also each of the six lines in each hexagram. This makes such a substantial body of art that the effect is immersive and captivating.

The result of this illustrative approach to the *I Ching* makes these hexagrams both beautiful and accessible. This illustrated format works so well because the *I Ching* is essentially a series of dynamic concepts that are offered as verbal analogies. An analogy is by nature a dynamic image at work in the mind. These pictorial images help the mind to understand the hexagrams better at a fundamental level below words.

Analogy is embedded into the very brush strokes of the written Chinese language. Their character writing itself originated by symbolizing objects. In that language, the first principle of character writing was "**Imitating the Form.**" I will adapt a few examples taken from my book, *Tao of Chaos* Patterns: For instance, here is the Chinese character for man: See him standing on the ground with his arms down at his sides. This character imitates the form by showing a man with lowered arms. 人

To portray more abstract notions, a second principle developed that was called "*Pointing at the Thing.*" Here you see the man again, but now with his arms extended to symbolize the character big: He is showing us the measure of something big ... perhaps he is describing the fish that got away. Thus an image could be modified by a slight twist of the brush to suggest a new twist in meaning. 大

Below is the symbol for mouth: It is a square opening drawn with the loose analog flow of a brush rather than the sharp nib of a pen. 口

And this mouth can be modified to become the abstract idea of word:

Dashes above the mouth reveal a sketchy version of an extended tongue that is busily wagging with sounds as it talks. 言

This progression of graphic imagery demonstrates how the Chinese evolved a written language by modifying what was originally a simple imitation of form using pictorial analogies.

How might we draw something so abstract as trustworthiness or good faith? Why, let's have that man stand by his word—literally—to honor it. Below is good faith: It is formed by the man moved into a radical position to stand fast by his word. 信

This example illustrates the third principle of Chinese writing, which may be translated as "*Joining the Meanings.*" It links one picture with another to suggest a new condition. Western languages sometimes do something similar to create a striking image—for example, we say, "**He is leapfrogging the issue**"—but our Western metaphors make images sketched by chunks of alphabet, not inked together by pictorial brush strokes.

Adele knows that today's woman might suppose that something so ancient as the I Ching, so locked in its customary language of a rural tribe so long ago and far away, would have nothing to say to today's woman engaged in her modern life.

But such is not the case. And Adele wanted to show it using her art in visual and textual lines. She has the ability to tap into the essence of what a hexagram means in terms of the woman who is contemplating its lines, its images. These images and words will of course speak to each age garbed in the vernacular and mindset of its time. Yet Adele sought to find the common denominator beneath the flow of change. For the eternal flow of the *I Ching* is deeper than its words, than its images. It rests in the dynamic patterns that shape the most fundamental and primal architecture of our universe.

This universal architecture is designed by patterns that the ancient Chinese recognized long ago, in fact, starting in 3322 BCE according to their historical documents. But the modern day scientist is only now beginning to recognize these patterns and call them by a different name—complexity theory.

In complexity theory, events that seem to be random chaos are actually composed of myriad patterns embedded in space, time, matter, and energy. They cycle on scales large and small, they are nested in each other like Russian dolls, and they evolve in patterns that are self-similar yet not exactly the same. It means that you get slight variations on a theme repeatedly. This is what gives nature the ability to be stable in its basic laws yet evolve in its presentation of everyday events. Time is still time, for instance, but it brings you something new each day.

This patterning organizes the very code that builds us, the DNA that shapes our bodies, bone, muscle, and skin. And it organizes our psyches too.

The genetic code in DNA is based on chaos patterning. That same DNA code—modern discovery that it is—can be found in the ancient mathematics of the I Ching. Modern geneticists have proved that DNA codes for our fleshly matter, while the ancient Chinese said the *I Ching* shows the flow of universal mind that can guide us more surely on our path by consulting its oracle.

And these two systems, ancient and modern, parallel each other both in logical math and in metaphysical meaning. I have written about this correlation between modern genetic structure and the *I Ching* symbolism in my book, *Tao of Chaos,* the first in a series of three books that probe just how deeply this code is embedded in nature. My second book, *Touching God's TOE,* deals with this chaos patterning code at the fundament of creation—embedded in the very shape of spacetime and twanging the superstrings that form matter and energy. Mind and matter—where do they meet? Right here in the *I Ching* shorthand.

It was Adele's interest in each nuance of the *I Ching* that brought us together and allowed me the chance to see her work. My breath was taken away by the beauty and subtlety of her images, by the layers of symbolism in their design, as well as by the womanly wisdom that whispered in the text itself.

This book is no slapdash effort to get a product out. It is the long-time fruition of her contemplative and artistic genius, and for that reason, I invite you to taste of its fruit and enjoy the savor. May this book lead you into contemplations of your own that make your life better, more satisfying, more grounded in the wisdom beyond words.

As an old adage in Taoism states, *"The Tao that can be spoken is not the Tao."* I feel sure that if you go through this volume of images and words carefully, you will acquire a far greater sense of emotional connectedness to the I Ching's first sixteen hexagrams and their meaning.

Katya Walter

Preface

A the time of this writing when I checked the list for *I Ching* books on Amazon.com there were 8,089 results for books in print and 193 published in eBook format on The Kindle. With that in mind, this is not the place for me to try to explain in any depth what this philosophy is that has captivated my interest for the past 40 years.

I have read a number of those books listed and include a small bibliography of some that I found useful. I will say that the Princeton University Press edition, translated by Richard Wilhelm, is still my favorite and is the interpretation that got me hooked into the *I Ching* in the first place. The Wilhelm interpretation of the *I Ching* was first published in 1950 and remains at the top of Amazon seller list for books about the I Ching. I especially recommend Carl Jung's foreword in this book for anyone who is not familiar with the *I Ching* and want a good introduction for understanding this ***Book of Changes***.

While this book of my *I Ching* inspired interpretations does not attempt to explain the scope of the history or philosophy of the *I Ching*, my hope is that my work can be enjoyed by both *I Ching* devotees and those who have not yet encountered the *I Ching*. For that reason I have to give some explanation of what the *I Ching* is so that new comers to the *I Ching* can have some perspective on my work.

What is the I Ching?

The *I Ching* or, ***Book of Changes*** has only one law that remains constant: The only thing that never changes is change itself.

I Ching is a philosophy and tool for divination that dates back to the origins of Chinese civilization; evolving along with the development of Chinese writing and culture. *I Ching* philosophy is organized around an inter-play of symbols derived from the elements of nature. It is a philosophy of right living based on the premise that everything in the universe arises out of two forces — Yang and Yin, the Chinese words for creative and receptive energy or masculine and feminine forces. The philosophy is that if you follow the way of nature you will find the right way and right time for action or non-action in your own life.

I Ching is often used as a tool of divination for aligning one's self with those elemental forces so that one may "swim the way the river is flowing."

In Carl Jung's foreword to the Wilhelm interpretation he mentions that he experienced the *I Ching* as a method for exploring the unconscious. Since the *I Ching* developed over centuries of Chinese civilization this ***Book of Changes*** has become a part of the collective unconscious.

Jung tells us that the Chinese mind has a completely different orientation of thought from our Western way of perceiving an event. In brief; the Western way of thinking is based on cause and effect. The Chinese mind, he says, is almost exclusively preoccupied with the chance aspect of events. When Jung wrote his foreword to the *I Ching* he helped introduce to the Western mind the concept of synchronicity, a phrase he coined and is widely used today.

The power of the *I Ching* is only activated through the interaction of the human mind. The archetypes in the *I Ching* were programmed over many centuries by the continual input and evolution of many human psyches. Therefore the *I Ching* reflects a collective response to the human condition as a part of nature. By consulting the *I Ching* as a tool of synchronicity we recognize ourselves as part of nature and that the universe and we are one organism.

I Ching Symbols

I Ching is the quintessential symbol book of all time, containing layers of symbols, one within the other. Symbols are used to describe other symbols. It is no wonder that people find this book of wisdom obscure. Because the nature of a symbol always points to something beyond itself, the meanings can never be pinned down but are always open to each new reader.

In one of the layers of symbols the *I Ching* projects attributes of personality and character onto the images of nature. These symbols also denote members of the archetypal family, body parts, direction and color association.

The *I Ching* is comprised of 64 situations, all derived from the combination of 2 lines, yang (whole) ▬▬▬ and yin (opened) ▬ ▬.

There are 4 combinations of the 2 lines. When the yin and yang lines are combined in sets of 3 they form the 8 trigrams. Each trigram is named for a force in nature and has other attributes associated with it. When the trigrams are combined in sets of 2 they form the 64 possible combinations that form the hexagrams.

The 8 images of nature that the *I Ching* is based on are: Heaven, Thunder, Water, Mountain, Earth, Wind/Wood, Fire and Lake.

The Trigrams and Symbolic Associations

Trigrams	Attribute	Animal	Body	Family	Direction	Color
☰ *Ch'ien • Creative Heaven*	Creativity Strength	Dragon & Horse	Head	Father	Northwest	Indigo
☳ *Kên • Arousing Thunder*	Action	Dragon	Feet	Eldest Son	East	Green
☵ *K'an • Abysmal Water*	Danger	Pig	Ear	Second Son	North	Black
☶ *Chên • Keeping Still Mountain*	Stillness	Dog	Hand	Youngest Son	Northeast	Purple
☷ *K'un • Receptive Earth*	Receptivity	Mare & Cow	Belly	Mother	Southwest	Yellow
☴ *Sun • Gentle Wind & Wood*	Penetration	Fowl	Thighs	Eldest Daughter	Southeast	Scarlet
☲ *Li • Clinging Fire*	Brightness Dependence	Pheasant	Eye	Second Daughter	South	Crimson
☱ *Tui • Joyous Lake*	Joy Pleasure	Sheep	Mouth	Youngest Daughter	West	White

The origins of the *I Ching* pre-date literacy. We can not begin to imagine today what it was like to live in an environment that did not include the Internet, telephone, electricity — you name it — and be solely dependent upon nature. The people of prehistoric China had to have respect for and awe of nature that in many ways has been lost to our consciousness today. The ancient Chinese did not see themselves as separate from the environment in which they lived.

Trigram • *Ch'ien* • The Creative Heaven

Trigram • Chen • The Arousing Thunder

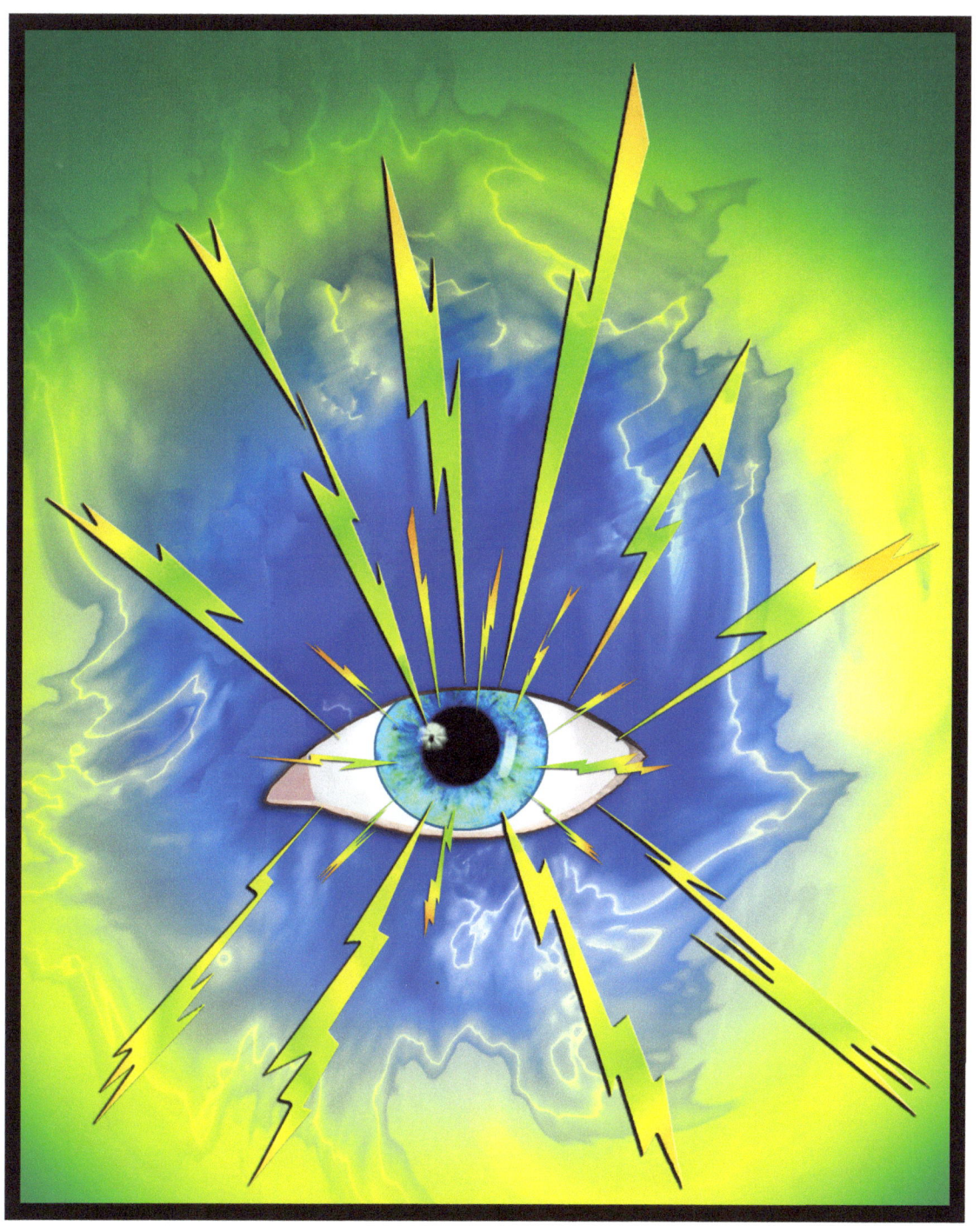

Trigram • *K'an* • The Abysmal Water

Trigram • Ken • The Keeping Still Mountain

Trigram • *K'un* • The Receptive Earth

Trigram • Sun • The Gentle Wind & Wood

Trigram • *Li* • The Clinging Fire

Trigram • *Tui* • The Joyous Lake

 *1 • Ch'ien • The Creative • Heaven over Heaven*

Hexagram 1 • *Ch'ien* • The Creative

Living *The Creative*
I experience the unfolding of time.
I am aware of the order in the universe,
Knowing that creation is change,
Transformation and continual movement.
I bring my potential into being.
I am successful and know that what I am doing
Comes from beyond myself through my Self.

A doubled Heaven is strength and power and duration.
I know that after each creation a new one will follow.

NINE IN THE FIRST PLACE

I am like a hidden dragon and cannot act. My creative force is still within.
I am not yet recognized. I remain true to myself, uninfluenced
By failure or success while I wait for my own ripe time.

 1 • Ch'ien • The Creative • Heaven over Heaven

NINE IN THE SECOND PLACE

I am like the light, like a dragon in my chosen field.
I am reliable, influencing my environment without conscious effort.

 1 • Ch'ien • The Creative • Heaven over Heaven

NINE IN THE THIRD PLACE

Creatively active all day, at night I am restless.
Others sleep while I am anxious.
In transition from lowliness to heights of recognition
I must be aware of the demands and pitfalls of the dawning time.

 1 • *Ch'ien* • *The Creative* • *Heaven over Heaven*

NINE IN THE FOURTH PLACE

Wavering flight . . .
I have reached a transition where free choice is possible.
I can be important in the world or stay my private self.
I listen to my soul and do what is right for me.

 1 • Ch'ien • The Creative • Heaven over Heaven

NINE IN THE FIFTH PLACE

I am like a Heavenly Dragon
...Flying...
My creations are seen in the world with blessings to all.

 1 • Ch'ien • The Creative • Heaven over Heaven

NINE IN THE LAST PLACE

A warning!
I must not be arrogant in my climb.
If I try to fly beyond my power I will fall and become isolated.

Hexagram 2 • *K'un* • The Receptive

I feel the pulsing rhythms of matter
In space which is Nature.
I bring completion to creativity
Which is the light power of consciousness,
Thinking and seeing.
Receptivity has the dark power of what is inside,
Unconscious and invisible.
What I cannot see may feel threatening.
By yielding
The dark mystery is revealed.

While my creative spirit soars to *Heaven* with energetic ideas.
I am receptive to absorb them.
To give birth to the unborn
I must nourish what is inside with devotion.

 2 • K'un • The Receptive • Earth over Earth

SIX IN THE FIRST PLACE

Frost . . . Followed by ice.
My own winter is inevitable.
Do I think that I can stop it?
Cold . . . Dark . .. Death?

 2 • K'un • The Receptive • Earth over Earth

SIX IN THE SECOND PLACE

My Heavenly spirit is like a circle with no idea of ending.
My Earthly Self is square, feeling boundaries and limits.
When I am receptive to my creativity
I am aware of my life pattern and become centered.

2 • K'un • The Receptive • Earth over Earth

SIX IN THE THIRD PLACE

When bringing creativity to birth or being of service to another
My work is hidden like a tree that knows fruit will bear in summer.
During this process I remain free of vanity
Letting beauty develop quietly within . . . Undisturbed.

2 • K'un • The Receptive • Earth over Earth

SIX IN THE FOURTH PLACE

I protect the unborn, a "tied up sack"
Carefully hiding, not yet ready
To live in the world.

 2 • K'un • The Receptive • Earth over Earth

SIX IN THE FIFTH PLACE

Golden . . . Reliable . . . Genuine like Earth,
Prominently pregnant, I meditate in discreet reserve
On the "child" dependent within.

 2 • K'un • The Receptive • Earth over Earth

SIX IN THE LAST PLACE

"Dragons fight in black and yellow blood!"
I am swollen and exhausted. What has been protected within the dark
Is breaking through in great force to live and breathe in the light.
I feel warning signs. The bloody battle to death or birth begins.
"Dragons fight in black and yellow blood!"

 3 • *Chun* • Difficulty at the Beginning • Water over Thunder

HEXAGRAM 3 • *CHUN* • DIFFICULTY AT THE BEGINNING

The Creative and Receptive unite
Giving birth to my individuality.
After the storms of confusion
And the darkness of not being
The newly born depends on help.

Like a seed,
I unravel the code to my uniqueness.
With nature as my guide
I struggle to grow and blossom,
Filling the world with new creations.

After flowering
My task is to let go of the parents of my past
So that I can grow into my new future.

 3 • *Chun* • *Difficulty at the Beginning* • *Water over Thunder*

NINE IN THE FIRST PLACE

In the beginning when things are still stormy
I cannot force growth.
I humbly await my time and then seek help.

 3 • *Chun* • *Difficulty at the Beginning* • *Water over Thunder*

SIX IN THE SECOND PLACE

I feel hindered when I experience many difficulties.
Every event seems sudden and unexpected.
I wait for a new growth cycle.

 3 • Chun • Difficulty at the Beginning • Water over Thunder

SIX IN THE THIRD PLACE

I cannot force events ahead of their time.
The seeds of my desire will mature in the future.

 3 • *Chun* • *Difficulty at the Beginning* • *Water over Thunder*

SIX IN THE FOURTH PLACE

I seek help.
The seeds of individuality need more nourishment
Before they can grow to their power of full development.

 3 • *Chun* • *Difficulty at the Beginning* • *Water over Thunder*

NINE IN THE FIFTH PLACE

While seeds have bloomed in multiplicity
What I have created is misunderstood.
Others project views of themselves onto me.
The truth wills out and difficulties turn into blessings.

 3 • Chun • Difficulty at the Beginning • Water over Thunder

SIX IN THE LAST PLACE

When difficulties become difficult ties I feel like giving up.
I must remember that like the birds feeding on the sunflower
I have many seeds and only one is needed to recreate myself.

 *4 • Mêng • Youthful Folly • Mountain over Water*

Hexagram 4 • *Mêng* • Youthful Folly

After discovering my individuality
I express myself
Like a bubbling spring.
I grow and learn
In the exuberance of Youthful Folly.

Youth is the fool of innocence.
Life is my teacher, the plan of nature.
Sometimes I question the obvious
And receive no answers.

My cocoon of youth in metamorphosis
Explodes in transformation and new awareness.

 4 • Mêng • *Youthful Folly* • *Mountain over Water*

SIX IN THE FIRST PLACE

In order to move through the leaves of life,
I abandon my confining egg of protection
As I become serious and disciplined while learning.

4 • Mêng • *Youthful Folly* • *Mountain over Water*

NINE IN THE SECOND PLACE

With the strength of youth and little knowledge
I am tolerant to what is hidden and undeveloped.
My true power unfolds into a larger and freer self
After I absorb and transform experience into character.

 4 • Mêng • *Youthful Folly* • *Mountain over Water*

SIX IN THE THIRD PLACE

Traveling along the way I meet another whom I admire.
I am not tempted to lose myself
By following a path that is not my own.

 4 • Mêng • *Youthful Folly* • *Mountain over Water*

SIX IN THE FOURTH PLACE

I am caught in the web of my imagination
Which entangles and prevents movement.
It is humiliating foolishness to be so trapped
When life forces me to struggle . . . unaided.

 4 • Mêng • *Youthful Folly* • *Mountain over Water*

SIX IN THE FIFTH PLACE

I see the mistakes I made in ignorance
And seek help so that I can fly
In my own direction.

4 • *Mêng* • *Youthful Folly* • *Mountain over Water*

NINE IN THE LAST PLACE

It is better to avoid a temptation
That brings punishment and pain.

5 • *Hsü* • Waiting • Water over Heaven

HEXAGRAM 5 • *HSÜ* • WAITING

Waiting is to discover
The destiny of the Self.
I wait with patience and courage
To see and accept the truth
Of who I am without illusion.
This waiting becomes a strength
That lights my path
To the right way of action.
I am guided by dreams,
The dark secret chambers of the soul
Which are like the rain clouds
That pour hidden knowledge into consciousness,
Bursting forth only when my psyche is ready.

While waiting I can nourish my fate
In moments of rest
When I eat and drink
And enjoy it all.

 5 • Hsü • Waiting • Water over Heaven

NINE IN THE FIRST PLACE

Awake . . . I wait . . .
Like an open meadow absorbing strength for future use.

 5 • Hsü • Waiting • Water over Heaven

NINE IN THE SECOND PLACE

I become like the sand that waits near the waters
Of my unconscious, pulling me nearer
To the dangers of what I fear
In that unknown pit.

 5 • Hsü • Waiting • Water over Heaven

NINE IN THE THIRD PLACE

Waiting in the mud
My mind is a murky water-earth mixture.
On the brink of dream shadows
I feel the hidden enemies of my soul.

5 • *Hsü* • *Waiting* • *Water over Heaven*

SIX IN THE FOURTH PLACE

I sink into the abyss of the unseen.
Is this life? Is this death?
I fall into the bloody pit of anxiety
. . . Released . . .
When I accept my fate and wake to reality.

 5 • *Hsü* • *Waiting* • *Water over Heaven*

NINE IN THE FIFTH PLACE

Restored by nourishment
I rest between moments of struggle
To enjoy peace in the awareness of now.

5 • Hsü • Waiting • Water over Heaven

SIX IN THE LAST PLACE

I fall back into dream, host of the uninvited.
I am afraid and then I accept this call of the soul, my **Fate**.
I welcome those unknown selves who surprise and foretell.
My dream within a dream becomes a vehicle for transformation
As the symbols surface to consciousness.

Hexagram 6 • Sung • Conflict

Conflicting needs pull me down
Into deep waters.

Weakened by conflict
Life becomes a mirror of different selves
Fighting for expression.
I pause to seek guidance.

Through introspection
I turn to my own wisdom in meditation.
When I can listen to all voices
I restore myself to harmony
And can act without conflict.

6 • *Sung* • *Conflict* • *Heaven over Water*

SIX IN THE FIRST PLACE

When I hear the first hum of those inner voices
I do not speak them.
I don't admit that a conflict exists.

 6 • *Sung* • *Conflict* • *Heaven over Water*

Nine in the Sectond Place

I do not blame others
Nor tell them of my doubts.
I retreat into the conflict of my inner self.

6 • *Sung* • *Conflict* • *Heaven over Water*

SIX IN THE THIRD PLACE

When my work is worn like a crown of creativity
I find who I am in the reflection
Of the other's mirror.

 *6 • Sung • Conflict • Heaven over Water*

NINE IN THE FOURTH PLACE

The more I resist my conflict the stronger it becomes.
. . . Finally . . .
I accept what I do not like in myself
And submit to this truth.

6 • *Sung* • *Conflict* • *Heaven over Water*

NINE IN THE FIFTH PLACE

At the peak of conflict
I seek guidance from my higher self.

6 • Sung • Conflict • Heaven over Water

NINE IN THE LAST PLACE

All that I resist persists!
When I cannot dissolve a conflict I project it onto others.
And then I am bound to meet it
As I see my face in theirs.

7 • *Shih* • *The Army* • *Earth over Water*

Hexagram 7 • *Shih* • The Army

I am like an army in battle
For the next frontier of the Self.
I maintain discipline as one area of my life
Is sacrificed for the attainment of another.
I am convinced of the value of this task.

I focus in one direction
As latent aspects of personality emerge
From the waters of my unconscious.
I marshal my strength
To bring this drama of inner life
Into objective reality.
When I am in command of myself
I can lead others.

After I achieve my goal
I am restored to balance
And live peacefully
In this hard-won new domain of my soul.

 7 • Shih • The Army • Earth over Water

SIX IN THE FIRST PLACE

I become organized
So that I can gather the strength
Needed for the battle force of discipline.

 7 • Shih • The Army • Earth over Water

NINE IN THE SECOND PLACE

I set my sights on achieving my goal.
Like a general, I am in command of the strength
Of my various selves.

 7 • Shih • The Army • Earth over Water

SIX IN THE THIRD PLACE

I have allowed myself to get out of control,
Causing a setback in my direction.

 7 • Shih • The Army • Earth over Water

SIX IN THE FOURTH PLACE

Overwhelmed in struggle
I retreat —
Gathering strength for future action.

7 • Shih • The Army • Earth over Water

SIX IN THE FIFTH PLACE

Many opportunities present themselves in the field of my endeavor.
I combat temptation to be led astray by anything less
Than achieving my highest goal.

7 • Shih • The Army • Earth over Water

SIX IN THE LAST PLACE

The struggle for discipline has been won.
Now my fighting instincts needed for that battle have become peaceful again.
I return to a more diffuse and orderly self
To live in the newly won territory of my soul.

8 • Pi • Union • Water over Earth

HEXAGRAM 8 • *PI* • UNION

After being disciplined
I become a strong focused mandala of being.
I am like the ocean
Containing all the rivers of my life.
Feeling my own inner union,
I attract that which I am.
I join with others in certainty.

When I hesitate the group unites without me.

8 • *Pi* • *Union* • *Water over Earth*

SIX IN THE FIRST PLACE

Loyally holding to my own truths
I am a vessel receiving the waters of life.
I receive without holding.

8 • Pi • Union • Water over Earth

SIX IN THE SECOND PLACE

I do not seek what does not seek me.
I look inward and am held there.

8 • Pi • Union • Water over Earth

SIX IN THE THIRD PLACE

I am free from attachment until I find what belongs to me.
I am wrong for those who are wrong for me.

8 • *Pi* • Union • Water over Earth

SIX IN THE FOURTH PLACE

I have found what centers me
As I openly show my devotion to that union.
What I want wants me.

8 • Pi • Union • Water over Earth

NINE IN THE FIFTH PLACE

Union seeks me.
Those meant to join see that I am like an open gate.
Those I love
Love me.

8 • *Pi* • *Union* • *Water over Earth*

SIX IN THE LAST PLACE

Those I did not join did not join with me.
I lose my head and can only envision
What might have been.

 *9 • Hsiao Chu'u • Taming power of the Small
Wind & Wood over Heaven*

HEXAGRAM 9 • *HSIAO CHU'U*
THE TAMING POWER OF THE SMALL

I am the restraint of the tension
In the moment before it all happens.
I am the power of one's shadow.
I am a seed in germination.
I am moisture in diffuse suspension
Before the cloud bursts.
I am the force in the wind
Gathering the rain.
I am the forgotten dream
That influences the day.
I am the moment before the full moon.
I am the spirit of Wind in Heaven.

9 • Hsiao Chu'u • Taming power of the Small
Wind & Wood over Heaven

NINE IN THE FIRST PLACE

I return to the way
My way!

 9 • *Hsiao Chu'u* • *Taming power of the Small*
Wind & Wood over Heaven

NINE IN THE SECOND PLACE

I am drawn back to where I belong.

*9 • Hsiao Chu'u • Taming power of the Small
Wind & Wood over Heaven*

NINE IN THE THIRD PLACE

I am stopped in an atmosphere of tension.

*9 • Hsiao Chu'u • Taming power of the Small
Wind & Wood over Heaven*

SIX IN THE FOURTH PLACE

I face anger storm that rage inside
And see that my angel wings are casting sword shadows.

9 • Hsiao Chu'u • Taming power of the Small
Wind & Wood over Heaven

NINE IN THE FIFTH PLACE

I experience excitement in the act of joining
And the pleasure of receiving in the giving.

9 • *Hsiao Chu'u* • *Taming power of the Small*
Wind & Wood over Heaven

NINE IN THE LAST PLACE

Release . . .
The moment of the fullest!
Then . . .
The cycle returns to the descent of what is now in power.

Hexagram 10 • *Lü* • Treading

The contained power of restraint
Is released and I am treading
Into manner and mode of expression.

Using a creative spirit
With joy and humor
I develop personality.
I accept my varying
And unequal levels of character traits
By giving them expression
In appropriate ways.

Moving with strength
While treading carefully
I handle unknown dangers
By allowing my thinking to be led
By deeper intuitions.

I protect myself
While pleasing others
And walk with the mask of a tiger.

 10 • Lü • Treading • Heaven over Lake

NINE IN THE FIRST PLACE

Tiger like
I move surely on the path
. . . Alone.

10 • Lü • Treading • Heaven over Lake

NINE IN THE SECOND PLACE

Looking straight ahead
I go deeper into a dark tiger-self
As my instincts show the way.

 10 • Lü • Treading • Heaven over Lake

SIX IN THE THIRD PLACE

I stumble and do not see clearly when I am swallowed by my persona.
In the weakness of fear my mask of aggression engulfs me.

 10 • Lü • Treading • Heaven over Lake

NINE IN THE FOURTH PLACE

I feel the strength of my powerful animal instincts.
I take care not to confuse myself with the mask of a tiger.

10 • Lü • Treading • Heaven over Lake

Nine in the Fifth Place

I am aware of my wildness
And move with it.

10 • Lü • Treading • Heaven over Lake

NINE IN THE LAST PLACE

Success in movement is like a hunt or a dance.
Power is in the process.
Quality of performance is the result of the care in each step taken.
The tiger, the path and I are one.

11 • T'ai • Peace • Earth over Heaven

HEXAGRAM 11 • *T'AI* • PEACE

After moving like the dance of a tiger
I realize I AM
That which I have been seeking.
I am in harmony with
Natural rhythms of being.
I express my highest creativity.
I am in the center of love,
The orgasmic flowering of my soul.
As each love blooms in the peace
Of its own nature — in its own time,
I feel completion
In this fusion of the opposites.

 11 • T'ai • Peace • Earth over Heaven

NINE IN THE FIRST PLACE

I am the roots and the earth
Created by the decay of past blooms.
Only time creates the illusion that soil and flower are not one.

 11 • T'ai • Peace • Earth over Heaven

NINE IN THE SECOND PLACE

I walk in the middle.
I am not lured into remaining any one smaller part of my being.
I trust my soul to lead me to wholeness.
I accept imperfections, recognizing all phases of life as functions of growth.

 11 • T'ai • Peace • Earth over Heaven

NINE IN THE THIRD PLACE

My space exists in the context of limits.
The boundaries of my being are defined by my inner nature.
Centered in awareness, I feel the thrust of growth in the process of change
And that all life is defined by death.

 11 • T'ai • Peace • Earth over Heaven

SIX IN THE FOURTH PLACE

Slowly . . .
I approach wholeness
As the polarities within begin to unite.

 *11 • T'ai • Peace • Earth over Heaven*

SIX IN THE FIFTH PLACE

A marriage of the Creative and Receptive
Produces the flower of my psyche,
The seeds of my soul in the peace of love.

11 • T'ai • Peace • Earth over Heaven

SIX IN THE LAST PLACE

Within the laws of change Peace turns to stagnation.
I move to a higher knowing by letting go as
These seeds fall from the center
To create the new.

12 • P'i • Standstill • Heaven over Earth

HEXAGRAM 12 • *P'I* • STANDSTILL

The flower of creation dies and I fall
From peace into stagnation.
This natural process follows the decay
Of the product of union.
I die to the world and go inward.
I am numb. I am a shadow.
I am hidden and confused.
I am unconscious and see no light.

It would help me at this time
To know I am a seed at the beginning
Of a new awakening.
Yet . . .
I am so much a part of this experience
I cannot see.

In the blackness of transformation
I stand still.

 12 • *P'i* • *Standstill* • *Heaven over Earth*

SIX IN THE FIRST PLACE

I am the roots and the earth created by the decay of my past blooms.
Only time creates the illusion that soil and flower are not one.
I die to the senses and find inner light.

 12 • P'i • Standstill • Heaven over Earth

SIX IN THE SECOND PLACE

I do not know who or where I am.
I force myself to trust isolation as necessary to a new awakening.

 12 • *P'i* • *Standstill* • *Heaven over Earth*

SIX IN THE THIRD PLACE

I am ashamed of my weakness,
Fear in isolation . . .
Crisis in the dark!

12 • P'i • Standstill • Heaven over Earth

NINE IN THE FOURTH PLACE

The time is right.
My highest essence guides me to the light again.
I open and find that I am not alone awakening.

 12 • P'i • Standstill • Heaven over Earth

NINE IN THE FIFTH PLACE

Moving from darkness into light I am blind in fear
That I have not the strength to flower.
Slowly . . . I become aware and realize my soul is as organic as all life,
My re-birth as mysterious and inevitable as death.

 12 • *P'i* • *Standstill* • *Heaven over Earth*

NINE IN THE LAST PLACE

I work consciously to return to creativity.
In that darkness of standing sill I discover
Stagnation and creation are two parts of the whole,
Each always moving into the other.

 13 • *T'ung Jên* • Open Friendship • Heaven over Fire

Hexagram 13 • *T'ung Jên*
Friendship in the Open

After standing still
I come out of black stillness
Like the flowers returning to new life.

I am one of many
As we reach to join in community.
We embody strength in character
When no one is the authority.

Our ideas are made brilliant
By joining the flames
Of our inner visions
As we share the experience
Of love within friendship.

13 • T'ung Jên • Open Friendship • Heaven over Fire

NINE IN THE FIRST PLACE

We form a gate to friendship
As we meet in the open
Without secrets.

 13 • *T'ung Jên* • *Open Friendship* • *Heaven over Fire*

SIX IN THE SECOND PLACE

When paired in exclusivity
We form a barrier to the larger community.

 13 • *T'ung Jên* • *Open Friendship* • *Heaven over Fire*

NINE IN THE THIRD PLACE

We hide from ourselves the mistrust we see in each other.
These thorns of doubt prevent us all
From picking the bouquets of friendship.

 13 • *T'ung Jên* • *Open Friendship* • *Heaven over Fire*

NINE IN THE FOURTH PLACE

We climb the wall of the barrier to friendship
Only to find all our doubts are mirrored back
And see that we cannot attack.

 13 • *T'ung Jên* • *Open Friendship* • *Heaven over Fire*

NINE IN THE FIFTH PLACE

We cry in the frustration of separation.
Our thoughts have met when our words said the opposite.
Our hearts have heard what our ears have not.
This truth breaks all walls, exploding into the open
With the joyous fragrance of our laughter.

 13 • *T'ung Jên* • *Open Friendship* • *Heaven over Fire*

NINE IN THE LAST PLACE

Before meeting in heartfelt relation
We join a community without expectation.

 14 • *Ta Yu* • *Possession in Great Measure* • *Fire over Heaven*

HEXAGRAM 14 • *TA YU*
POSSESSION IN GREAT MEASURE

In the controlling grace
Between fate and time
The power of the Self awakens.

Alive in the experience
My visions are created
From the inside out
Bringing riches of realization

Sight and Insight —
Illumination of imagination.
Can I possess more than this?
Fire in Heaven!

 14 • *Ta Yu* • *Possession in Great Measure* • *Fire over Heaven*

NINE IN THE FIRST PLACE

I see the dark and the light
With the insight that precedes creativity.

 14 • *Ta Yu* • *Possession in Great Measure* • *Fire over Heaven*

NINE IN THE SECOND PLACE

As the energy of the opposites unite
I become a vehicle for mobility of power
And my dreams and reality move in one direction.

 14 • *Ta Yu* • *Possession in Great Measure* • *Fire over Heaven*

NINE IN THE THIRD PLACE

I sacrifice all that I know
To my soul's higher vision.

 14 • *Ta Yu* • *Possession in Great Measure* • *Fire over Heaven*

NINE IN THE FOURTH PLACE

As I ride on the back of time
Progressing in my soul's journey,
I know the difference between the riches of others
And my own destiny.

 14 • Ta Yu • *Possession in Great Measure* • *Fire over Heaven*

SIX IN THE FIFTH PLACE

I trust the integrity of my soul.
With this dignity I always possess all that I give away.

 14 • Ta Yu • Possession in Great Measure • Fire over Heaven

NINE IN THE LAST PLACE

By following my soul's desire
I have been rewarded and blessed.
I humbly honor that Sun-bird light of heaven.

 *15 • Ch'ien • Modesty • Earth over Mountain*

Hexagram 15 • *Ch'ien* • Modesty

After experiencing the treasure of the Self
I see a destiny to my life's events.

I do not seek the heights and risk of the new
But bow to what I know.

What had been a struggle becomes easy.

I am simultaneously aware
Of the insignificance of my own existence
And that there is no molecule
In this universe not equal to the whole.

I am lifted up by bowing down in modesty.

 15 • *Ch'ien* • *Modesty* • *Earth over Mountain*

SIX IN THE FIRST PLACE

As I begin a task I remain humble,
Bending to my ground of experience.

15 • Ch'ien • Modesty • Earth over Mountain

Six in the Second Place

I find no problem when I speak from my heart.

15 • Ch'ien • Modesty • Earth over Mountain

NINE IN THE THIRD PLACE

The secret to success is to complete my task
Before seeking praise for that which is still potential.

 15 • *Ch'ien* • *Modesty* • *Earth over Mountain*

SIX IN THE FOURTH PLACE

As the work grows I become more accomplished
And I learn to accept responsibility.

 15 • *Ch'ien* • *Modesty* • *Earth over Mountain*

SIX IN THE FIFTH PLACE

I am forced to take a stand.
Modesty is not passivity but assurance of the way to reach one's goal with integrity.

15 • Ch'ien • Modesty • Earth over Mountain

SIX IN THE LAST PLACE

My task is not complete.
With all my strength I reach again with modesty.

Hexagram 16 • Yü • Enthusiasm

After experiencing a modest possession of my Self
My energy is lived in movement
With a release from tension
Like an electric storm in Spring.
This thunder is the music of reawakening life.

I am in awe for all creation.
I sing and celebrate the past sounds from the sea,
The future dance of the cosmos
Whirling in rhythmic regularity.

I seek my natural place
Where there is least resistance
Arousing enthusiasm in others
By playing my song in their way.

16 • Yü • Enthusiasm • Thunder over Earth

SIX IN THE FIRST PLACE

When I first feel enthusiasm
I wait, holding back expression.

16 • *Yü* • *Enthusiasm* • *Thunder over Earth*

SIX IN THE SECOND PLACE

When I can listen to sounds of the past
That point to the seeds of the future
I gain knowledge without illusion.

 16 • *Yü* • *Enthusiasm* • *Thunder over Earth*

SIX IN THE THIRD PLACE

Now is the time! I do not hesitate.
Enthusiasm grows in the twists of fate.

16 • *Yü* • *Enthusiasm* • *Thunder over Earth*

NINE IN THE FOURTH PLACE

The secret of enthusiasm in gathering others
Comes from clarity and freedom from doubt
About myself and them.

 16 • *Yü* • *Enthusiasm* • *Thunder over Earth*

SIX IN THE FIFTH PLACE

Enthusiasm always meets with resistance
Which becomes the material that shapes my way.
Stretched to my limits, tired and tense
I am propelled on in the origin of the movement of enthusiasm.

16 • *Yü* • *Enthusiasm* • *Thunder over Earth*

SIX IN THE LAST PLACE

I let go of enthusiasm, lifting my thoughts from the shell of the past.

History of my art inspired by the I Ching.

When I first encountered the *I Ching* it was a translation that I couldn't understand. I put the book aside. Then in 1970 I happened to be reading a lot of Carl Jung and read his forward to the *I Ching* at the same time I was reading the letters between Lawrence Durrell and Henry Miller in which Miller mentioned his interest in the *I Ching*. That did it! I bought the Princeton edition with the forward in it by Jung and have been hooked ever since.

It was also at this time that I became involved with the Woman's movement. While both the Woman's movement and the *I Ching* helped to change my life many feminists asked me how could I be interested in a book that was so sexist? This question was thrown at me so often I then decided that I would create an interpretation from a woman's point of view. Of course since then many thousands of books have been written about the *I Ching* and some of them by women.

Since I am an artist I then decided to create a visual interpretation, including my own words, for this wonderful *I Ching, Book of Changes*. This decision turns out to have been an act of hubris on my part. I though it would take me a few years to complete — a ridiculous assumption! All kinds of life interruptions stopped my progress and on the way I made many changes to my own *Book of Changes*.

Back in the dark ages before the Internet and development of the personal computer, I began my *I Ching* inspired art with a set of black and white abstract woodcuts integrating astrology symbols with the trigrams. I made 64 prints that I laminated onto canvasses and strung them all together in a large wall construction.

I also made two sets of these prints on rice paper and hand bound them into books, 16 X 20" in size. After that I made a similar set in color and created a limited edition book called, *Changes.*

Next I translated these designs into large acrylic paintings 36" X 48." These were all in an exhibition in the Greenwich Connecticut library in 1972. No one in the library at that time knew what the *I Ching* was but Nixon had just opened up communication with China so they were interested in having this show.

I acquired an old press where I hand set with old fashioned lead type a limited edition letterpress set of folders for Hexagrams One, Two and Three.

I moved from Connecticut to California in 1976 and earned a Ph.D. in "Art and The Personal Symbolic Process" from The Union Institute University in 1981. The work included some of my illustrations and writings from *I Ching Meditations,* as well as a study of dreams.

In my next version of *I Ching Meditations* I created black and white pen and ink drawings for hexagrams one through sixteen. They were photocopied as a limited edition book in 1983. I worked with José Argüelles as my core professor for my PhD at The Union Institute University. José was also another *I Ching* enthusiast and graciously wrote a foreword for that limited edition.

In 1984 I was introduced to the Macintosh computer, literally at the moment of its birth. I wrote a review for the program, *Mac Paint,* for A+ Magazine. *Mac Paint* was the program that helped sell this new revolutionary computer. We had all of 18k of Ram, the screen was tiny, and the images could only be created in black and white. But I could draw and print my images on this new computer. I instantly saw the potential in what this new tool could do as a medium for art and publishing. And when the Macintosh was upgraded to include color I began making more changes to my work, translating the black and white drawings into color.

The next big event for changes was the arrival of the Internet. So it was a logical next step to put *I Ching Meditations* on line where I have been slowly completing the latest version of my *Woman's Book of Changes.*

With the ever changing development of the computer graphic programs Photoshop, Illustrator, Flash, Poser, Bryce, and more, it becomes a life's work just to keep up with the technology. I decided, **STOP!** Finish what I started over 40 years ago and publish what is now complete before I decide that for some unforeseen reason I have to begin again. With this book now finalized in print — on to Volume 2 and the next sixteen hexagrams.

Adele Aldridge
December 14, 2012

BIBLIOGRAPHY

Cleary, Thomas (Translator) Lui I-Ming (Author). *The Taoist I Ching.* Boston, MA: Shambhala Publications 1986.

Cleary, Thomas. *I Ching Mandalas: A Program of Study for The Book of Changes.* Boston, MA: Shambhala Publications 1989.

Hook, Diana Ffaringto.. *The I Ching and Mankind.* London and Boston: Routledge & Kegan Paul Ltd 1975.

Hook, Diana Ffarington. *The I Ching and You.* New York, NY: E. P. Dutton 1973.

Karcher, Stephen. *Total I Ching: Myths for Change.* London, England: Little, Brown Group 2008.

Lynn, Richard John. *The Classic of Changes: A New Translation of the I Ching as Interpreted by Wang Bi.* New York, NY: Columbia University Press 1994.

Ritsema, Rudolf and Stephen Karcher. *I Ching: The Classic Chinese Oracle of Change: The First Complete Translation With Concordance.* New York, NY: Barns & Noble, Inc., Element Books 1995.

Smith, Richard J. *The I Ching A Biography.* Princeton, NJ: Princeton University Press, 2012.

Smith, Richard J. *Fathoming the Cosmos and Ordering the world: The Yijing (I Ching, or Classic of Changes and Its Evolution in China.* Charlottesville and London: University of Virginia Press 2008.

Wilhelm, Helmut (Author) Cary F. Baynes (Translator) *Changes: Eight lectures on the I Ching.* New York, NY: Bollingen Foundation by Pantheon Books. Inc. 1960.

Wilhelm, Richard, Cary F. Baynes, Hellmut Wilhelm and C. G. Jung. *The I Ching or Book of Changes,* Bollingen Foundation, New York, NY: by Princeton University Press, Princeton, NJ 1967.

Walter, Katya. *The Tao of Chaos: Merging East and West.* Austin, TX: Kairos Center 1994.

About the Author

Adele Aldridge has been working with the *I Ching* for 40 years as a learner and as an artist creating images and text for *I Ching Meditations — A Woman's Book of Changes.* She earned a Ph.D. in Art and the Personal Symbolic Process, studying with José Argüelles at the Union Institute University. She has thirty-five years of experience as a fine artist showing her work in galleries in New York, Connecticut and San Francisco, and has worked as a Book Illustrator, Graphic Designer, Web Designer and Instructor in Computer Graphic programs. You can learn more about Adele Aldridge's work with the *I Ching* at: www.ichingmeditations.com.

About Katya Walter

Katya Walter has an interdisciplinary Ph.D. She spent 5 years of post-doctoral study at the Jung Institute of Zurich, and a year of post-study in China. Dr. Walter taught in colleges and universities in the USA and abroad for sixteen years before focusing on writing, lecturing, and workshops. Dr. Walter is author of the *Touching God's TOE* series of books.: Vol. 1: *Tao of Chaos: Merging East and West.* Vol. 2: *Double Bubble Universe*, Vol. 3: *The Universe is Alive & Well*, Vol. 4: *The Universal Fractal Tree*, Vol. 5: *Fractal Gravitons*, Vol. 6: *Quantum Organics.* She also authored *Dream Mail,* a handbook on the fractal messages carried in the deeper structure of dreams. Her web site is http://doublebubbleuniverse.com

www.ingramcontent.com/pod-product-compliance
Lightning Source LLC
Chambersburg PA
CBHW041532220426
43662CB00002B/36